Entertaining
ASIAN STYLE

Entertaining
ASIAN STYLE

DECORATING IDEAS AND MENUS

by Lisa Kim-Tribolati and Martyne Kupciunas
Photography by Peter Mealin

PERIPLUS

contents

authors' preface 9 **a style both old and new**

introduction 10 **entertaining today**

the houses . **the food**

in living color 16 **mediterranean pleasures**

form & feng shui 24 **fragrant rice and rolls**

the comfort zone 36 **pacific rim cuisine**

pretty in pink 46 **high tea**

a touch of zen 54 **asian appetizers**

the pool house 64 **sushi and cocktails**

java style 74 **an indonesian buffet**

asian accents 84 **curried flavors**

ethnic chic 92 **cajun to asian**

a moonlit courtyard 100 **twilight supper**

indigo night 112 **fabulous finger food**

appendix 122 **tips, conversion table and index**

Published by Periplus Editions (HK) Ltd.,
with editorial offices at 5 Little Road #08-01, Singapore
536983 and 153 Milk Street, Boston MA 02109

Publisher: Eric Oey
Creative Director: Christina Ong
Editor: Melanie Raymond
Design: Loretta Reilly
Production: Mary Chia, TC Su

Acknowledgments:

Thanks to Tom Kupciunas, who continues to amaze me
with his patience and understanding. M. K.
To John, Hong, Flora, and Susan. L. K.

Special thanks to Peter Mealin, for magically capturing
our ideas and words in his photography, and for his and
Choai Leng's patience, faith, and friendship. Thanks to
Loretta Reilly, for her imagination and creativity; to
Melanie Raymond, the best editor and friend with
whom we were blessed; to Eric Oey, for his guidance
and wisdom; and to Christina Ong, for her exceptional
vision and unflappable support.

Many thanks to old and new friends who let us into
their homes, shared ideas and recipes, and really made
this book possible: Lucena Austria; Lucia Boey; Chan
Soo Khian and SCDA Architects; David Droga; Carol
Dunning; Stephen Falatko; Mary and Robert Franklin;
Franz Friedl; Gan Jai Hong; Gan San San and Jacinta
Gomes; Geh Min and Tong Ming Chuan; Terry and
Robert Gibralter; Lyn and Mike Hall; Richard Helfer;
Lincoln and Muffin Hoffman; Sandra Jarvis; Amy
Katoh; Elizabeth and Chris Lin; Mark and Jamie
Loveland; Burke and Cary McKinney; Philip Norfleet;
Louis Phun and Colonial Home; Mrs Ong; Diana and T.
K. Quek and Quek Associates; Emi Querubin;
Magdeline Shaw; Leonie and Jean-Marie Simart; and
Thomas Winslade.

Distributors:

Japan: Tuttle Shokai Inc.,
Tama-ku, Kawasaki-shi, Kanagawa-ken 214-0022

Asia: Berkeley Books Pte. Ltd.,
5 Little Road #08-01, Singapore 536983

USA: Charles E. Tuttle Co. Inc.,
RRI Box 231-5, North Clarendon, VT 05759-9700

A style both old and new

Pink, jade, turquoise and lemon: the elegant facades of terraced houses shimmer in the heat of the afternoon sun. Louvered wooden shutters are tightly shut against the glare while on the ground floors, the ornate *pintu pagars*, or half doors, guard the privacy of the occupants while allowing tropical breezes to enter. Welcome to Emerald Hill Road, Singapore.

When we moved to Singapore we were both lucky enough to find ourselves living in the renovated shophouses that fringe this colorful road. Shophouses are a traditional form of terraced house built early this century in the Malay Peninsula by the Peranakan communities (descendants of the Chinese traders who married Malay women). The interior spaces of these historic homes are long and narrow; on average, shophouses are just 18 feet wide. The open or enclosed central courtyards let in light and are perfect for the more casual style of entertaining encouraged by the equatorial heat.

This relaxed, leisurely style of entertaining exemplifies what we have come to think of as "the new Asian style", and inspired us to write this book. In the modern Asian home, the traditional furnishings and flavors of the Orient are infused with a Western sense of freedom and whimsy. In the realms of both food and decor, tradition has been spiced up with humor and a knack for the creative combination has replaced the formal. Inexpensive paper Chinese lanterns are coupled with rare and exquisite porcelain, and an airy lychee mousse might follow a piquant Cajun gumbo; all served on a fresh banana leaf. In today's international kitchen, cilantro and ginger are as much a necessity as olive oil and garlic.

Above all, the essence of this new style of decor and entertaining is a sense of balance and serenity; modernity is now at ease with tradition. This tranquility is also at the heart of life on Emerald Hill Road. Walking down this street you can imagine what life was like when this area was a nutmeg plantation. Children still play on the street and at night, the scents of different cuisines linger in the jasmine trees. Dainty bats dance in the light of the five-foot walkways. As for the cats of Emerald Hill Road . . . they are a book on their own.

Entertaining today

"Have you eaten today?" is a heartfelt Asian greeting, reflecting the importance of food not only as fuel for the body but for the well-being of the soul. In cities such as Singapore, Hong Kong and Bangkok, eating is a 24-hour pastime indulging all the senses, from the pungent aroma of fresh *chai* (tea) and breakfast noodles at daybreak, to the sound of fragrant *laksa* (seafood soup) being enthusiastically slurped at alfresco hawker stalls in the wee hours of the morning.

To dine together as family, friends or business colleagues is to establish and strengthen bonds—rarely is a business deal struck without feasting. As in the West, most socializing is done in restaurants and hotels, so an invitation to someone's home is an honor— just as it is an honor to host such a special occasion. Equal attention is lavished on presentation and preparation; both of the food itself and of the surroundings, so that they enhance the overall dining experience.

the occasion

There seems to be a festival on any given day of the year in Asia, where excuses to celebrate are as plentiful as lotuses in a temple pond. Look beyond Thanksgiving and Christmas and celebrate Chinese New Year, a Thai water festival, or a Balinese temple festival. Or relish the harvest seasons by welcoming the blossoming of spring flowers or the arrival of the first tender stalks of asparagus or succulent strawberries to the stores.

Whether the meal will be formal or informal, sit-down or buffet-style, a multi-course feast or a cocktail party, will be determined by the size of your guest list.

the decor

The aesthetics of your surroundings are determined more by your imagination and time than budget. If you are traveling in Asia, immerse yourself in specialty shops bursting with bargain baskets, fabrics for tablecloths, curios and conversational pieces. Closer to home, stroll through your neighborhood Chinatown and other ethnic shops in your area for interesting and inexpensive crockery, containers and objects to add a distinctive touch to your table and home. Or find new uses for treasures you already possess. In one

of the homes we visit, an old Japanese keyaki wood warehouse door is resurrected as an eye-catching tabletop. Silken cushions in saturated shades add exuberance to outdoor furnishings. The following pages will show you a multitude of uses for utensils and accessories from Indonesia, Japan, China and India, from wine coolers and ice buckets to floral containers and candleholders.

Concentrate on the rooms your guests will occupy, including the bathroom. Scented candles, a small flower or potpourri arrangement—perhaps in an incense holder or basket—and hand towels placed in a rustic wooden bowl exude atmosphere and luxury.

flower power

From religious offerings to personal adornment, tropical flowers are intrinsic to the Asian lifestyle. Available in abundance in their native habitats, they may be sourced inexpensively in the West from wholesale florists or Asian grocers. Exotic varieties such as the Bird of Paradise are striking sculptures in their own right; a single Casa Blanca lily makes a strong statement on an elegant table. A few stems of night-blooming jasmine or frangipani cast a net of intoxicating fragrance over an entrance hall or courtyard. In the West, the flowers usually take precedence over the container but in Asia, containers evoke fascinating vignettes of their own. White orchids spill like rice grains from an antique Thai basket; a Cambodian silver box cradles a treasure of roses and silver beads. Flowers often unfurl overnight so can be arranged the day before your occasion.

mood lighting

Asian evenings are suffused with the pungent aroma of incense and the heady scent of votive candles. Naked torches flare along balmy beachside walkways; a red paper lantern glows surreally in an inner-city temple entrance. Recreate the magic and theatre of the Orient in your home by placing candles in a betel-nut box or translucent fish lanterns in a kaleidoscope of rainbow hues. Be careful not to set scented candles too close to food as they may overpower its natural aroma.

left *Chill your best champagne in large terra-cotta bowls filled with ice.*
top *Hand towels are placed in a wooden bowl for the bathroom.*
above *An attractive arrangement of fresh fruit provides a thoughtful and welcoming touch for a guest's bedroom.*

in living color

mediterranean pleasures

Fashionable lemon-lime and turquoise hues streak happily across this living room. Inspired by the saturated colors of the tropics, the vibrant and sophisticated fabrics used here add zest and excitement to their surroundings.

If you have always opted for a beige and cream color scheme and are a little hesitant about introducing strong, bold colors, start with patterned pillows, cushion covers or a tablecloth. Paint a guest bathroom in dazzling colors or drape a bright scarf over your favorite chair. Try personalizing your own linen. We stenciled gold geckos on white and gold-trimmed linen napkins. They add an element of surprise to a table setting and are an amusing and creative alternative to plain napkins.

With all this vivid color to occupy the eye, decorations are kept to a minimum. Large tropical flower arrangements provide all the interest here; not only are they colorful, but their unusual shapes and sizes add drama to a room. A single, well-placed flower or leaf may be all you need to accent a corner. Here we've displayed heliconia in a large glass vase; a graceful Mokoyama leaf is used to hide the stems.

This relaxed Mediterranean-style lunch for family or friends was inspired by the color scheme. Glossy red and yellow bell peppers filled with caponata are served on a cobalt blue dish. The dishes here can all be prepared the night before and served at room temperature, which makes them wonderfully versatile.

far left *Sunflowers add a dash of color to a platter of beef tenderloin. Think about shape as well as color when choosing flowers, the gold and yellow tones of these sunflowers and tulips may be similar but the different shapes provide contrast.*

left *The simplicity of a glass vase works best for some floral arrangements. To prevent water from getting cloudy, add one teaspoon of liquid bleach per quart of water.*

below *Fresh fruit, as appealing to look at as to eat, is the main ingredient of dessert. The whimsical gecko napkins featured here were stenciled especially for this lunch. See page 122 to find out how to stencil your favorite design on your own napkins.*

form & feng shui

fragrant rice & rolls

left *A cantilevered stair-case, magically suspended in the air like a huge sculpture, descends to the ground floor.*

This elegant home is a play on form, function and *feng shui*. *Feng shui*, the ancient Chinese art of placement, holds that the proper placement of furniture and objects will greatly enhance the flow of *chí i*, or energy, and bring prosperity to the prudent occupants of the *feng shui* building.

Everything in this architect's home flows in perfect harmony. The monochromatic color scheme was chosen to expand the long narrow space imposed by the structure of the shophouse. This subdued background also serves to highlight the Southeast Asian paintings hanging on the wall. In fact, the house was built to showcase the family's much-prized collection of Asian art, which includes rare and exquisite sculptures as well as paintings. It is obvious that careful attention was paid to the positioning of each piece—whether in deference to the art of the geomancer or just the art itself. An otherwise stark wall on the first floor provides the perfect backdrop for the drama of the traditional Japanese wedding kimono. The elegance of its design and the subtlety of the fabric's colors and textures are just some of the aspects of its beauty.

"Good fortune" is the theme of the dining room featured on page 31, hence red, considered an auspicious color in Chinese culture, is the keynote color of the decor. The shapes and colors used in the lantern festival painting are echoed in this table setting for a formal lunch. Traditional Chinese plates decorated with dragon motifs symbolizing prosperity are placed on the red paper fans which are an exotic alternative to placemats. Inlaid enamel chopsticks rest on pewter fish and the Winter Cherry flowers used as the floral centerpiece repeat the lantern shapes in the painting. Gold Chinese lunar calendar animals are scattered around the table for more good luck and to add a quirky and personal touch. In contrast to the refined opulence of the setting, lunch is classic Singaporean hawker stall food: Popiah (a version of fresh spring rolls), and the ubiquitous and much loved Hainanese Chicken Rice.

above *A rare Chinese stone frieze decorates a wall of the indoor pond. Koi, the good luck fish, play beneath the surface.*

right *This stunning glass dining table is a collector's item. An antique Chinese drum made of leather and brass fittings has been put to ingenious use to create the base of the table.*

previous pages *The beautifully designed staircase cuts a strong vertical swathe through the dining room. The functional elements of this home have been considered as carefully as the decorative ones.*

For lunch, dishes synonymous with Singapore were chosen: Popiah and Chicken Rice. Popiah are the Singaporean version of fresh spring rolls and have been modified here so they can be served as a first course. In case the authentic wrappers are hard to find, we also used crepe wrappers, shaping them into small packets stuffed with the filling. Chicken Rice is simplicity itself, consisting only of poached chicken and aromatic rice flavored with chicken stock. Serve with chili sauce for an added punch of flavor. Following the main course, fresh fruit and nuts dipped in chocolate are served near the tranquil *koi* pond. If you prefer to continue with the Chinese menu, serve egg custard tarts bought from a Chinese bakery.

easy *popiah*

ingredients
filling
2 tablespoons vegetable oil
4 cloves garlic, minced
1 pound pork loin, cut into very thin strips
3 cups finely sliced jicama
1 cup finely sliced carrots
1 cup water
1 tablespoon oyster sauce

for wraps
60 (5 x 5-inch) frozen spring roll wrappers or
45 (8 x 8-inch) crepes
Hoisin sauce
1 1/2 cups bean sprouts
1 cup snow peas, blanched, refreshed, and finely chopped
3/4 pound small shrimp, cooked and chopped
1/2 pound Chinese sausage, steamed for 20 minutes, cooled, and thinly sliced

45 scallions, green part only, blanched and refreshed in ice water

Heat the vegetable oil in a skillet, add garlic and cook for 30 seconds, stirring constantly. Add pork and cook until no longer pink, about 3 to 5 minutes. Add jicama and carrots and cook for 5 minutes, stirring constantly.

Add water and oyster sauce and bring to a boil. Reduce heat and simmer uncovered for about 25 to 30 minutes, stirring occasionally, or until jicama and carrots are tender and most of the water has evaporated. The mixture should still be moist. When cooked, remove the vegetable-pork mixture from heat and let cool.

For the popiah wraps:

If using spring roll wrappers, defrost and keep covered with a damp tea towel to prevent wrappers from drying out. Take one wrapper and cut into 3 equal strips. Lay a wrapper on your work surface with one of the corners toward you. Place one strip across the center of the wrapper. (You will need 4 wrappers for every 3 rolls.) Spread 1/2 teaspoon of hoisin sauce on the center strip. Top with a tablespoon or so of the pork mixture. Then scatter some bean sprouts, snow peas, shrimp, and sausage over the filling.

Fold the corner closest to you toward the far corner but stop about an inch short of the corner. Then fold the right corner over the center followed by the left, making sure they overlap. Take one scallion, gently wrap around the roll and tie to hold the roll together. Repeat with the remaining wrappers and ingredients. Keep the finished popiah covered with a damp tea towel until ready to serve.

If using frozen crepes (as shown here), defrost, and using a 6-inch diameter pastry cutter, cut circles out of each crepe. Keep the crepes covered with damp tea towel to prevent them from drying out. Follow the instructions above, using 1 teaspoon of the hoisin sauce, 1 1/2 tablespoons of the filling and slightly more of the individual toppings. If using crepes, there is no need to add the extra strip as the crepes are already sufficiently thick.
Makes 45 popiah packets.

note: *Pork-vegetable mixture can be made a day ahead and refrigerated. The other ingredients can also be prepared a day ahead and refrigerated. The rolls can be made an hour in advance but should be kept covered with a damp tea towel at room temperature.*

Easy Popiah.

chili sauce

ingredients

^{1}/4 cup chopped red chili pepper (remove the seeds and
inner membrane if you prefer a milder sauce)
4 cloves garlic, sliced
4 tablespoons rice vinegar
1 tablespoon sugar, or more to taste

Put all the ingredients into a blender and purée.
Makes about ^{1}/3 cup.

note: *Chili sauce can be refrigerated in a glass jar for up to a week.*

chicken rice

ingredients

chicken

6 chicken breasts on the bone, with skin
Salt
5 quarts water
1 (6-inch) piece ginger, cut into 1-inch thick slices and bruised with the side of the knife

rice

1 tablespoon sesame oil
2 cloves garlic, minced
1 tablespoon minced fresh ginger
3 cups long-grain rice, rinsed and drained
6 cups chicken stock from above
$1/4$ teaspoon salt

garnish

Cucumbers, tomatoes and cilantro (optional) for garnish

To cook the chicken:

Season the chicken breasts with salt and rub it in. Let sit for 15 to 30 minutes. Bring the water and ginger to a boil in a large stock pot. Add the chicken breasts and bring to a second boil. If the chicken is not entirely covered with liquid, add more water. Reduce heat to a simmer, cover and cook until chicken is done, about 20 minutes.

Remove the chicken from the pot. Reserve 6 cups of the cooking liquid for the rice. Skim the fat from the surface of the chicken stock and set aside. When ready to serve, debone the cooled chicken breasts and slice crosswise into smaller pieces.

For the rice:

Heat the sesame oil in a pot. Add garlic and ginger and sauté for 1 minute, taking care not to burn the garlic. Stir in the rice and sauté for 1 minute, constantly stirring so the rice is coated with the oil.

Add the chicken stock and bring to a boil. Cover pot, reduce heat to low and simmer until rice is tender and the liquid absorbed, about 20 minutes. Remove the pot from the heat and let stand for about 10 minutes without removing the cover.
Serves 6.

presentation: *Pack rice firmly in a bowl, place a plate over the bowl and overturn the bowl onto the plate. Carefully remove the bowl to unmold the rice. Arrange the chicken slices around the side of the rice and garnish with sliced cucumber, tomato, and sprigs of cilantro. Serve with chili sauce (recipe page 33) and dark soy sauce in bowls on the side.*

notes: *The chicken can be cooked a day ahead. Refrigerate chicken and reserved stock to cook the rice. If you plan on cooking rice often, an electric automatic rice cooker is a must-have appliance; it cooks perfect rice every time. They are inexpensive and can be found at Asian markets.*

Chicken Rice.

chocolate *dipped fruit*

ingredients

1/2 pound of good-quality dark or milk chocolate, chopped
Your choice of a variety of fruit, such as whole strawberries, slices of apple, pear, kiwi fruit, or banana
Your choice of whole shelled nuts, such as pistachios, macadamia, walnuts, hazelnuts, cashews or almonds

Place chopped chocolate in a heat-proof bowl and place over another bowl of hot water. Stir chocolate until melted.

Dip half the piece of fruit or fruit slice into the chocolate and swirl to cover. Place on baking sheets lined with parchment paper. Continue with remaining fruit. Refrigerate to set.

For the nuts:
Spread nuts out on baking sheet lined with parchment paper. Transfer chocolate into piping bag and pipe chocolate over an individual nut until covered. Continue with remaining nuts. Refrigerate to set.

note: *If chocolate begins to stiffen, place the bowl over hot water.*

the comfort zone

pacific rim cuisine

As work encroaches ever further into our leisure time and technology changes the way that we do business, home has become an extension of the office for many people, if not the office itself.

Carved wooden doors from Thailand lead the way into this multifunctional home that allows the owner to host a dinner for clients as easily as relax in front of the television set with the family. While the first consideration for the design of this interior was comfort, the challenge was to maintain the intimacy of a family environment while recognizing the owner's desire to conduct business at home. The highback wing chairs, comfortable classic sofas and golf memorabilia are combined to create an atmosphere of ease and leisure, while the large dining-room table and board-room-like chairs add a necessary touch of corporate formality. The television set and stereo are cleverly housed in an attractive cabinet, allowing the owner to shut them away when the living room is being used for business.

As a change of pace from the anonymity of conference rooms and restaurants, this business lunch was brought home. For this purpose, a table setting which is sophisticated and formal enough for clients was needed. Crisply pressed white linen placemats and napkins, white china, and gleaming silverware are *de rigueur* corporate dining style and are complemented here with an eye-catching arrangement of bright tropical flowers (following pages). For the lunch menu, the delights of Pacific Rim cuisine are offered. Foods from the New World blend with exotic Asian produce and are prepared in a simple but stylish manner to highlight the fresh natural flavors of the ingredients.

39

pretty in pink

high tea

Afternoon tea is a rarity in today's busy world, a deliberate pause in the day for serenity and sustenance. It is a much-loved tradition that conjures romantic images of bygone days when tea and other luxuries from the Orient were traded in Europe and the New World. It is also one of the most enjoyable ways to entertain and unwind with friends and acquaintances.

Afternoon tea has never gone out of fashion at the grandest hotels, and with good reason. Its versatility allows you to adapt it to your needs: Plan a cozy and intimate gathering with good friends and lots of gossip; or present a lavish and opulent affair reminiscent of lazy afternoons and long white dresses.

Bring out your finest china and your best lace or linen tablecloth, and treat your guests to a variety of sweets and savories. Not owning a complete china or antique silver tea set should not stop you from hosting a high tea; mix and match with different pieces of china and silver found at flea markets or tag sales. The pretty buffet-style tea table here was created with touches from two great tea-drinking cultures: the English and the Chinese. Classic Wedgewood crockery and a grand silver tea service contrast with inexpensive Chinese napkin holders, and an antique Chinese screen depicting aristocratic ladies at a tea party affords an added note of gentility in the background.

Roses provide the perfect touch floral touch for your table; the soft charm of their pastel shades evocative of an English garden. This setting is as perfect a blend of East meets West as the tea that is being served, romantic unruffled elegance at its best.

For afternoon tea, serve a generous selection of sweet and savory tidbits. Instead of the traditional cucumber sandwiches, we served spicy curry and hearty beef puffs, open tuna sandwiches, and salmon ribbons. Cater to the sweet tooths among your guests with scones and preserves, which can be bought from any of the good bakeries in your area. Consider setting out a selection of tea leaves, such as Darjeeling, English Breakfast or Lapsang Souchong, in bowls, each clearly labeled. You may even want to break from custom and provide some herbal teas such as camomile, lemon-balm or mint. Provide a couple of pots of hot water and sugar, honey, milk, cream, and lemon wedges.

vegetable curry puffs

ingredients
2 tablespoons vegetable oil
1 large onion, diced (or about 1 1/3 cups)
2 cloves garlic, minced
1 teaspoon minced fresh ginger
2 cups cooked potatoes, peeled and cut into small cubes
1/2 cup fresh or frozen green peas, thaw if frozen
1 teaspoon ground coriander
1/2 teaspoon ground cumin
1/4 teaspoon ground turmeric
1/4 teaspoon garam masala
1/4 teaspoon cayenne, or more to taste
1/2 teaspoon salt
2 teaspoons fresh lemon juice
5 (10 x 10-inch) frozen puff pastry sheets

Heat the oil in a large skillet. Add onion and cook until soft, about 3 minutes. Stir in garlic and ginger and continue stirring for approximately 1 minute or until aromatic.

Add the cooked potatoes and cook for 5 minutes, stirring occasionally .

Stir in peas, coriander, cumin, turmeric, *garam masala*, cayenne and salt. Mix until all ingredients are well incorporated. Don't worry if some of the potatoes get mashed in the mixing process. Cook for about a minute. Remove from heat and add the lemon juice. Let potato mixture cool completely.

Preheat oven to 400 ° F.

Cut pastry into 3-inch circles with a pastry cutter. Take one circle of pastry and place about a teaspoon or so of potato mixture in the center. Bring the sides of the circle together over the filling and pinch the edges tightly to form a half circle. Repeat with the remaining potato mixture and pastry circles.

Place curry puffs on a baking sheet and bake until puffed and golden brown, about 15 to 20 minutes.

Makes 40 small puffs.

colonial tuna sandwiches

ingredients
1 cup solid white tuna packed in water, well drained (four 6-ounce cans)
1 tablespoon minced shallot
Dash of ground paprika
1/3 cup mayonnaise
Mini pita bread, or toasted white bread cut into 3-inch rounds, or toasted baguette slices
Chutney
Parsley leaves to garnish

Combine tuna, shallot, and paprika. Mix in 1/3 cup mayonnaise and add more until the desired consistency is achieved. Spoon 1 tablespoon of tuna mixture onto each mini-pita, toasted white bread or baguette, and top with 1 teaspoon of chutney of your choice. Garnish with parsley leaf.

Makes approximately 20 sandwiches.

note: *The tuna mixture can be made up to 2 days in advance and stored in the refrigerator.*

Colonial Tuna Sandwiches.

smoked *salmon* ribbons

i n g r e d i e n t s
ribbons
Cucumber
Smoked salmon, sliced thinly
Caper-cream cheese spread

caper-cream cheese spread
6 tablespoons cream cheese
1 tablespoon capers, drained and chopped
Makes about 6 tablespoons

Slice cucumber lengthwise into 20 thin slices with a mandoline or Japanese slicer. Trim the smoked salmon pieces to fit the cucumber slices.

Spread a cucumber slice with some caper-cream cheese spread and top with a slice of smoked salmon. Starting at one end, roll the cucumber and salmon slices and secure with a toothpick.

For the caper-cream cheese spread:
Mix cream cheese and capers together in a bowl. Refrigerate until ready to use.
Makes about 20 ribbons.

note: *The spread can be made a day ahead and kept in the refrigerator.*

spicy *madeira* *beef* puffs

ingredients

1 teaspoon vegetable oil
1 pound ground beef
1 tablespoon unsalted butter
1/2 large onion, finely diced
2 cloves garlic, minced
2 cups button mushrooms, thinly sliced
3 tablespoons Madeira
2 to 3 drops Tabasco, or more to taste
2 teaspoons Worcestershire sauce
1/4 teaspoon salt
Ground black pepper to taste
4 (10 x 10-inch) frozen puff pastry sheets, or 5 (10 x 10-inch) frozen puff pastry sheets for smaller puffs

Heat the vegetable oil in a large skillet. Cook beef for about 5 minutes or until brown, stirring constantly to break up large bits. Remove beef from pan with a slotted spoon and set aside.

In another pan heat the butter and add the diced onion. Cook until soft, stirring constantly, this should take about 3 minutes. Add garlic and continue stirring for 1 minute, taking care not to burn the garlic.

Add the cooked beef, mushrooms, Madeira, Tabasco and Worcestershire sauce, salt and pepper, and cook until mushrooms turn soft and the liquid has evaporated, about 5 minutes. Remove from heat and let cool.

Preheat oven to 400 ° F.

Cut a pastry sheet into 4 squares. Take one square and place 3 tablespoons of beef filling in the center. Form a triangle by folding one corner over to meet the opposite corner, and then press the edges together tightly. Continue with remaining ingredients.

Place puffs on a baking sheet and bake until pastry is puffed and golden brown, about 20–25 minutes.

For smaller puffs:

Cut a pastry sheet into thirds vertically, then into thirds horizontally, creating 9 squares. Take one square and place 1 tablespoon of beef filling in the center and continue as described above until you have used up all the ingredients. Baking time for smaller puffs may need to be reduced to 15–20 minutes.

Makes 15 puffs or 40 small puffs.

notes: *It is easier to work with the puff pastry if it is partially thawed, as the dough can sometimes be too soft to work with when fully thawed. Just place the pastry back in the freezer for about 5 minutes to stiffen the dough. Both curry and beef puffs can be made well in advance and frozen; a terrific standby for when those unexpected guests visit or you have a spontaneous cocktail party. When ready to serve, place the puffs in the oven without defrosting and bake for 15-25 minutes, depending on the size of the puffs.*

Spicy Maderia Beef Puffs.

puff pastry canapés

ingredients

Frozen puff pastry sheets
Your preferred topping: crème fraîche, caviar, smoked salmon and capers, cheese spread, ice cream

Keep a supply of puff pastry in your freezer for last minute canapés. Take a $2^1/2$-inch round cookie cutter and cut circles from a sheet of pastry. Place on a baking sheet and bake at 375 ° F for 10-15 minutes or until the pastry is golden and puffed up. Remove from the oven and, with your thumb wrapped in a tea towel to prevent burning yourself, gently press down on the center of the each puff. Fill the puffs with your topping of desire—crème fraîche and caviar, smoked salmon and capers; pipe in your favorite cheese spread; or for sweets, place a small scoop of ice cream in the center and cover with your favorite topping.

a touch of zen

asian appetizers

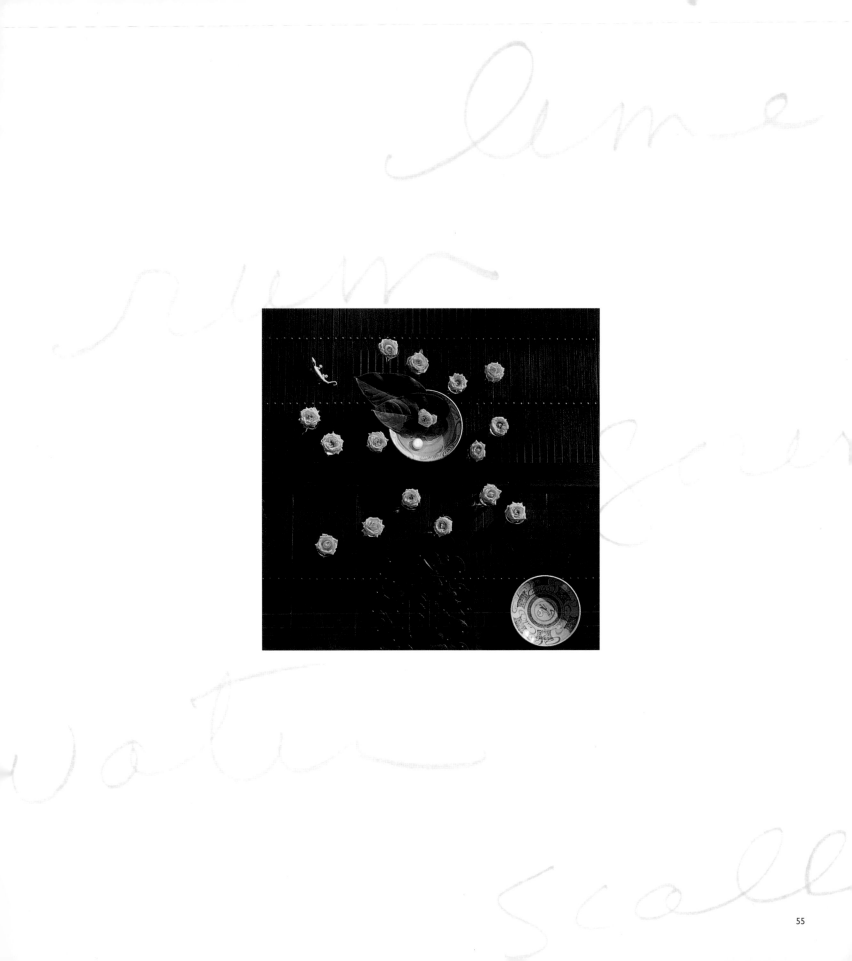

Inspired by the simplicity of Zen, this home is an example of uncluttered elegance. Simplicity of form, strong lines and bold compositions combine to form an interior that is balanced in shape as well as color and texture. Sculptured pieces of furniture and unique artifacts have been harmoniously arranged to utilize the narrow space in this Peranakan shophouse.

The subtlety of the decor and the clean lines of the furniture create an atmosphere of serenity, providing the perfect background for the rare and exquisite objects that have been lovingly collected from many parts of Asia—Burma, China, Indonesia and Japan, to name a few. Every object is a testament of the owners' longstanding fascination with the East and has its own anecdote, to be shared with visitors. The trunk of a large teak tree from Sulawesi, crafted into a coffee table, is nicknamed "King Kong" because it takes four people to lift it. Behind the table, three Japanese washi paper lamps rise up from the floor like illuminated sails, their delicacy emphasized by the rugged and earthbound qualities of the table. Although simple, this room is far from stark. The restrained decorating style enhances the beauty of the furniture and *objéts-d'arts*, which complement rather than compete with each other. If the furnishings in this interior are important, so too the spaces between them.

To create this relaxed and informal atmosphere for an evening of casual drinks with close friends, we lit candles nestled in a betel-nut box. A length of fabric from East Bali is draped over the table which has served as the focal point for many happy, impromptu social gatherings. In keeping with the simplicity of the surroundings, freshly prepared spring rolls are served because they can be eaten without the fuss of utensils. The hot pink gerberas, placed in a teak container which also doubles as an ice bucket, add a touch of exuberance to the occasion.

left *A 19th-century Ming-style bamboo jacket graces the wall and a Burmese lion coconut-husker watches over a tray of spring rolls. The iron balls from India were originally used to hold oil lamps; lighting the way of elephant keepers as they guided their herds at night.*

page 55 *Individual yellow roses in glass pebble vases rest like dew drops on the Keyaki wood table. Now a stunning feature of the living room, the table is in fact an old Japanese warehouse door, complete with original large doorlock hardware and wheels.*

above *The serene expression of the beautifully carved angel from Thailand casts a spell of tranquility over the room. White orchids and a silk shawl are draped over a Chinese merchant's jar, once used to store pickled vegetables or eggs.*

Irresistible spring rolls, a melange of subtle and exotic flavors, are served with a chili dipping sauce for a casual evening with friends. And the perfect cocktails to sip while enjoying the appetizers are refreshing soursop daquiries. The intriguingly named soursop, also known as guanabana, is a prickly, kidney-shaped fruit; its flavor is somewhere between that of mango and a pineapple. The Chinese classify soursop as a "cooling" fruit and it makes an ideal drink with which to quench your thirst on a hot, sticky summer day.

spring rolls

ingredients

filling

2 teaspoons vegetable oil
2 cloves garlic, minced
1 tablespoon finely chopped fresh ginger
1/2 pound lean ground pork
1/2 cup finely chopped scallions
1 cup canned water chestnuts, drained and chopped
1/2 cup crabmeat, fresh or canned, drain if using canned
2 tablespoons finely chopped cilantro leaves
2 tablespoons Chinese oyster sauce
1 tablespoon Thai fish sauce (nam pla)
Freshly ground black pepper to taste

25–30 (10 x 10-inch) sheets of spring roll wrappers, choose ones that do not contain egg
Vegetable oil for frying

To make the filling:
Heat vegetable oil in large skillet and add garlic and ginger, stirring until fragrant, about 30 seconds. Add pork and stir, breaking up meat into small bits. Cook until done or when pork loses its pinkness, about 3 to 5 minutes. Add scallions and cook for 1 minute. Remove skillet from heat and add water chestnuts, crabmeat, and cilantro to pork mixture. Mix oyster and fish sauces together and add to pork mixture. Add black pepper to taste and mix all ingredients until well incorporated.

To make the spring rolls:
Lay a sheet of wrapper diagonally on your working surface, with one of the corners facing you. Place a heaping tablespoon of filling horizontally across the lower third of the wrapper. Fold the corner closest to you over the filling towards the center. Roll once, gently but tightly, away from you. Fold the right corner over the center followed by the left and continue rolling away from you to completely enclose the filling. Moisten the last corner with water to seal. Let stand corner-side down.

To fry:
Pour vegetable oil into a heavy skillet to a depth of 1 inch. Set over medium heat until sizzling hot. Dip a wooden spoon in the hot oil; the oil should bubble and sizzle gently around the spoon when it is hot enough. Carefully place 4 to 5 spring rolls into the hot oil, taking care not to splatter the oil. Fry, turning several times until crisp and golden, about 5 minutes. Drain on paper towels. Let oil return to original frying temperature before adding a new batch of rolls to fry. Keep rolls warm by transferring them to a warm oven.

Serve warm with Chili Sauce, recipe on page 33.
Makes about 25 rolls, serves 6.

presentation: Wrap each roll in a Bibb or Boston lettuce leaf and tie together with the green portion of a blanched scallion. To blanch, dip scallions, trimmed of their white bulb end, into a pot of boiling water for about 15 seconds. Remove and plunge into a bowl of iced water to refresh; this stops the cooking process and sets the color. Pat dry with a paper towel. Blanching softens the scallions so they can be tied around the rolls and knotted without breaking.

Spring Rolls.

soursop *daiquiries*

For a fruit cocktail:

Peel the skin and remove the seeds from the fruit. Put the flesh into a blender or juice extractor with the lime juice, crushed ice and a little sugar syrup. Blend until smooth. Pour into glasses and serve.

For daiquiries:

Add rum and the Cointreau to the fruit cocktail above and blend a second time. Pour into glasses and serve. For mango daiquiries, simply substitute 4 mangoes for the soursop. Experiment with a wide variety of fresh tropical fruit such as kiwi fruit, watermelon, and papaya for non-alcoholic and alcoholic daiquiries.

Serves 4.

presentation: *Decorate glasses with slices of star fruit or dragon fruit.*

the pool house

sushi and cocktails

left *A unique living room: rest and relax or splash and swim. The narrow but long pool takes full advantage of the depth of the traditional shophouse.*

page 65 *This dramatic floral display is a good example of keeping it simple: agapanthus, a few sprays of wild orchid and a large leaf from the elephant ear plant—just add water.*

Water, water everywhere . . . A living room may not be the usual location for a swimming pool, but that is the delightful surprise that awaits you upon entering this unconventional but stunning home.

The occupants insisted on having an indoor pool, and the living room was the only possible location, given the typically deep and narrow structure of this renovated shophouse. In keeping with the clean lines of the room and the serenity of the water, simple furnishings were chosen to create an informal yet elegant oasis where it is possible to both entertain and cool off in the pool. The fabrics chosen for the cushions and furniture are strong and bright, adding warmth and color to an interior that is otherwise cool and minimal. The high ceilings and stark white walls are emphasized by the length of the graceful tropical plants that stretch their way up to the light.

Poolside entertaining, especially the outside sort, is a wonderful way to celebrate on hot summer evenings (or any evening if you live in the tropics). The pool itself offered a unique design opportunity for entertaining. Rather than trying to play down its presence, we decided to dress it up and turn it into a shimmering indoor lake. For a more structured floral arrangement than flowers floating on the water, we placed wild orchid and agapanthas on bamboo poles and stretched them across the water; the vivid yellow and purple hues of the flowers contrasting beautifully with the turquoise water. (This arrangement is also easy to remove for guests who want to swim.)

For a relaxed evening gathering of friends, we planned a menu that is both casual and stylish, and perhaps just a little unconventional: like the house itself. Sushi—simple yet always refined —is served with iced sake as cool and transparent as the water itself.

far left *A frozen sake bottle decorated with wild orchids. You can present all sorts of drinks in decorative frozen containers. See page 123.*

left *Platters of azure blue glass that evoke the sea are the perfect platters on which to serve sushi, the food of the sea. When serving Japanese food, try using crockery that contrasts in shape with the food you are serving.*

The hard-to-beat sophistication yet sheer simplicity of sushi was the inspiration for this menu. The easy to prepare dishes include fresh salmon with a sesame-soy dressing, pickled daikon maki, and cherry tomatoes stuffed with crabmeat. The important thing to remember when preparing raw fish is to buy impeccably fresh sashimi-quality fish from a reputable fish market and to have them pack it with dry ice to ensure its freshness on the ride home.

daikon *maki*

ingredients

3 sheets of toasted nori, *cut in half lengthwise or parallel to the lines on the seaweed*
2^1/2 cups sushi rice (see recipe on the opposite page)
1 long piece takuan *or pickled daikon radish, sliced lengthwise into 6 strips, each ^{1}/2-inch wide*

You will need a sushi mat made of strips of bamboo to shape the rolls. They are inexpensive and can be found in Japanese or other Asian markets.

Place the mat flat on your working surface. Place 1 sheet of the *nori* horizontally on the mat. The length of one end of the *nori* should be lined up with the bottom of the mat. Moisten your hands and spread a small handful of rice evenly over the *nori*, leaving an approximately ^{1}/4-inch band at the far end. Center a daikon strip horizontally across the sushi rice. Holding the daikon in place, lift the end of the mat closest to you and roll the *nori* over the daikon to meet the rice on the side farthest away. Adjust the roll into a teardrop shape by pinching the ends which meet tightly together.

Remove the mat and cut the roll in half crosswise. Then cut each half into thirds leaving you with 6 pieces. Repeat the process with the remaining sheets of *nori* and ingredients. *Makes 36 pieces.*

notes: Nori *are the thin sheets of dried seaweed commonly used in Japanese and Korean cuisine. They are sold in stacks of several sheets either toasted or untoasted. They can be found in Japanese and Korean grocery stores.*

Takuan is a daikon radish which has been pickled. It is yellow in color and has a sweet-sour flavor with a slight crunch. Sliced takuan is served as an accompaniment with Japanese meals. It is sold by the half piece in the refrigerated section of Japanese markets.

Experiment with various fillings using the nori *and sushi rice: strips of omelet, pieces of avocado, etc.*

Salmon Tartare (middle) and Daikon Maki (bottom).

sushi rice

ingredients

1 cup Japanese rice

2 cups water

2 tablespoons vinegar

1/2 tablespoon sugar

1 teaspoon salt

Rinse rice until water runs clear. Drain well and transfer to a saucepan. Add water and soak rice for 20 minutes. Bring to a boil, then reduce to a simmer, cover and cook for 20 minutes. Remove from heat and let sit for 20 minutes covered.

Mix together the vinegar, sugar and salt until the sugar has dissolved.

Transfer the cooked rice to a wide, nonreactive bowl and spread the rice evenly around the bottom and the sides. Sprinkle the vinegar mixture evenly over the rice, taking care not to add too much liquid (you may not need all of the vinegar mixture). Gently mix the rice with a large wooden spoon until vinegar mixture is well absorbed. Cover rice with a damp tea towel and let cool.

note: *Sushi rice can be made a day in advance and stored in the refrigerator, covered tightly with plastic wrap. Let the rice come to room temperature before using.*

71

sesame style salmon tartare

ingredients

3/4 pound fresh sashimi-quality salmon, skinned and boned
1 cup peeled, seeded and diced cucumber
2 tablespoons finely sliced scallions
1 tablespoon chopped cilantro leaves
2 tablespoons roasted pine nuts, finely chopped
1/4 cup sesame dressing
30 shiso leaves

sesame dressing

1 tablespoon sesame paste
4 teaspoons light soy sauce
1 tablespoon rice wine vinegar
1 tablespoon finely diced ginger
2 cloves garlic, finely diced
1 tablespoon fine sugar
1/4 cup sesame oil

For the salmon:
Cut the salmon into $1/4$-inch square pieces. Combine salmon, cucumber, scallions, cilantro leaves, pine nuts and sesame dressing (see below) in a bowl and toss until well mixed. *Makes about 30 hors d'oeuvres-size servings.*

For the sesame dressing:
Whisk together sesame paste and soy sauce in a bowl. Whisk in vinegar. While stirring, add ginger, garlic, and sugar, and stir until sugar has dissolved. Whisk in sesame oil. Let dressing stand for at least 30 minutes to allow the flavors to blend together.

presentation: *Place a tablespoon of salmon mixture on a shiso leaf or a lettuce leaf.*

note: Shiso *leaves, aromatic with a subtle minty taste, make a refreshing contrast to the richness of the salmon. They are a popular garnish on Japanese dishes and can be found in Japanese markets.*

cherry tomatoes stuffed with crabmeat

ingredients

30 cherry tomatoes, choose large ones
4 ounces crabmeat, fresh or canned, drain if using canned
1 tablespoon finely diced shallot
2 tablespoons cream cheese
Pinch of salt, to taste
30 avocado slices
Flying fish roe or caviar of your choice

Slightly trim the bottom of the tomatoes so they can stand. Cut the tops of the tomatoes and gently scoop out the seeds and flesh.

Mix the crabmeat, diced shallot, cream cheese, and salt together until all ingredients are well combined.

Stuff each tomato with some crabmeat mixture, top with a slice of avocado and some flying fish roe or caviar.
Makes 30.

preparation: *Use a $1/4$-inch diameter melon baller to hollow out cherry tomatoes. The tomatoes can be prepared and stuffed the day before. Top with avocado and roe just before serving as avocado flesh darkens when exposed to air. To prevent discoloration, sprinkle some lemon juice or vinegar on the exposed flesh.*

Cherry Tomatoes and Gari.

pickled ginger (gari)

ingredients

8 ounces young ginger

6 tablespoons rice vinegar

2 tablespoons mirin

2 tablespoons sake

5 teaspoons sugar

Brush the ginger under running water, then blanch in boiling water for 1 minute. Drain.

Put the vinegar, *mirin*, *sake* and sugar in a small saucepan and bring to a boil, stirring until the sugar dissolves. Allow to cool.

Put the ginger in a sterilized jar and pour the cooled vinegar over it. Cover and let ginger rest for 3–4 days before using. This will keep refrigerated for up to 1 month.

notes: *Pickled ginger, which will develop a pale pink color as it ages, is sliced and served with sushi. It can also be bought bottled from Asian grocery stores.*

Mirin is a rice wine used only for cooking; if it is not available, use 1 teaspoon of sugar as a substitute for one teaspoon of mirin. *Mirin is sold in bottles and can be bought from Asian grocery stores.*

java style

an indonesian buffet

left The living room, decorated with Chinese and Javanese furniture, provides the backdrop to a sumptuous platter of Indonesian finger food.

Open courtyards where the rain cascades down and an open kitchen are just two of the features that make this house so interesting. Rich wooden cabinets and other furnishings from East Java fit this open breezy space to a tee. The beauty of this furniture is such that you need only a few key pieces to decorate a room; the strong lines and warm patina of the finishes add drama to any setting. As the spaces are large and open, the furniture is used to define the living areas. Because of their size and durability, Javanese cabinets and furnishings are ideal for storage or entertainment centers, as well as looking fabulous on their own. Javanese furniture can be happily blended with interiors that are more Western than this tropical home; although, you will probably find that once you've added a few pieces, you'll want to continue with the Indonesian theme and add samples of the many wonderful fabrics, furnishings and sculptures that can be found all over the archipelago.

The style and spices of the South Seas blow freely through this home. In keeping with the unhindered flow of the living spaces, the entertaining style here tends to be both casual and progressive. We started with hors d'oeuvres in the kitchen and moved to the next room for a delicious buffet that samples the fragrant and fiery delights of Indonesian cuisine. The partially open kitchen is an inviting and informal space in which the guests gather to gossip, drink apéritifs, and keep the cook company while the evening's buffet dinner is prepared: a succulent array of satays, salsa and seafood. *Jodags*, the wooden lanterns from Java, are filled with candles; in the days before electricity, *jodags* were filled with oil and lit. Used here as rustic candleholders, they cast a flickering light over freshly cut coconut and flaming chilies.

These are the simple pleasures of life. Add a few banana leaves to the setting and you really could be in Java.

far left *The quintessential elements of Indonesian cuisine— the spice box and the coconut. Behind them are traditional Indonesian oil lamps or jodags.*

top left *The courtyard is an integral feature of the shophouse. Not only is it an ideal area in which to entertain, but encourages much needed evening breezes to flow through the house.*

below left *Hand-carved wooden tools are displayed on a long wooden chest that adds warmth and interest to an otherwise dull space beneath the stairs.*

79

This buffet contains a mouth-tingling array of textures and flavors from the Indonesian archipelago. Chicken and mushroom satays, succulent roasted squid, and cilantro crab cakes are served with peanut and chili sauces, while a sweet-sour pineapple and cucumber salsa offers a crunchy contrast. Although not Indonesian, we've added tortillas to the platter, providing you with the option of making your own rolls. The mild taste of the tortillas is a nice foil for the spicy flavors of the Indonesian food. Tortillas can be bought either fresh or frozen from your local supermarket. To heat, loosely wrap a stack of tortillas in aluminum foil and place in a warm oven for about 5 minutes. If you are using the frozen ones, allow them to defrost first.

cilantro crab cakes

ingredients

2 tablespoons diced shallot
3/4 cup cooked crabmeat (if using canned, drain thoroughly)
1/2 cup bread crumbs
2 tablespoons chopped cilantro leaves
2 eggs, lightly beaten
1 teaspoon Worcestershire sauce
Several drops Tabasco, to taste
Salt to taste

Combine the shallot, crabmeat, bread crumbs, and cilantro in a bowl. Mix the eggs, Worcestershire sauce, Tabasco and salt together in a small bowl. Stir the egg mixture into the crab and bread crumb mixture until everything is well combined, taking care not to break up the lumps of crabmeat. Form crab cakes into flattened rounds, each about 2 1/2 inches wide and 1/2 inch thick, and place on baking sheet. The crab cakes can be covered in plastic wrap and refrigerated for up to 4 hours at this point. When ready to cook, place the cakes in a preheated oven at 350 ° F and bake until golden brown, about 15 to 20 minutes.

Makes about 10 cakes.

presentation: *Serve all the dishes for this buffet together on a large platter covered with banana leaves. Freshly cut banana leaves make excellent natural serving platters and can also be used as placemats. Look for them at your local vegetable stand or in Asian markets.*

chicken satay

ingredients
marinade

2 cloves garlic, roughly chopped
2 onions, chopped
1 teaspoon curry powder
1 teaspoon ground cumin
1 teaspoon ground ginger
2 stalks lemongrass, chopped
(see preparation notes beneath satay sauce recipe)

1 pound chicken fillets

Place marinade ingredients in a small food processor and blend. Remove from the processor and add the chicken to the marinade. Marinate for 30 minutes.

Thread the chicken on skewers and cook on a hot grill.

Serve immediately with satay sauce.

Makes 10 skewers.

preparation: *If you are using wooden skewers for the satays, always soak them in water for several hours before placing them on the grill, to prevent burning.*

Chicken Satay (left), Satay Sauce (top) and Chili Sauce (bottom).

satay sauce

ingredients
2 tablespoons vegetable oil
12 shallots, finely chopped
1¹/2 teaspoons dried shrimp paste (blachan)
1 teaspoon cayenne
2 stalks lemongrass, finely chopped (see notes)
1 can coconut milk (10 fluid ounces)
2 tablespoons sugar
2 tablespoons chunky peanut butter
1 teaspoon salt
2 tablespoons chopped cilantro leaves

Heat the oil in a skillet and cook the shallots, shrimp paste, cayenne and lemongrass until fragrant, about 5 minutes.

Add the coconut milk, sugar, peanut butter and salt and cook, stirring constantly for about 10 to 15 minutes.

Remove from heat and stir in the cilantro leaves.

Makes about 1 cup.

preparation: *Lemongrass is a slim bulb with a lemony scent and flavor. To use, peel off the tough outer layers, cut away the top two-thirds of the stalk and trim the root end. Use the remaining third of the lower, tender portion of the bulb. Lemongrass needs to be finely chopped or pounded to release its fragrance.*

mushroom satay

ingredients
marinade
2 cloves garlic, minced
1 teaspoon fresh grated ginger
2 tablespoons cilantro leaves, chopped
3 tablespoons fish sauce (nam pla)
2 tablespoons sesame oil

20 shiitake mushrooms, stems removed

For the marinade:
Combine the garlic, ginger and cilantro leaves. Whisk fish sauce and sesame oil together in a small bowl and add to the garlic, ginger and cilantro mixture. Stir well.

Add the mushrooms to the marinade and coat well. Marinate for 1 hour.

Thread 2 mushrooms onto each skewer and cook on a hot grill.
Makes 10 skewers.

pineapple & cucumber salsa

ingredients
1 cup pineapple, sliced into small, thin pieces
1 cup Japanese cucumber, peeled and sliced into small, thin pieces
1/4 cup diced red onion (optional)
2 tablespoons rice vinegar
1 tablespoon sugar
1 small chili pepper, or more to taste, finely chopped

In a bowl, combine pineapple and cucumber pieces, and the onion if using.

In a small bowl, stir together vinegar, sugar and chili until sugar is dissolved.

Add vinegar mixture to pineapple-cucumber mixture and toss well.

Before serving, let salsa stand for 30 minutes at room temperature or up to 4 hours, refrigerated and covered with plastic wrap.
Makes 2 cups.

Main dish: Roasted Squid.

roasted squid

ingredients

2 tablespoons extra-virgin olive oil
4 cloves garlic, chopped
Salt and ground black pepper, to taste
1 pound squid, cleaned and cut in half lengthwise
2 tablespoons chopped cilantro leaves

Mix the oil, garlic and salt and pepper together in a small bowl. Add squid to oil mixture and toss until well coated.

Place the seasoned squid in a baking dish and roast in a preheated 450 ° F oven until squid is cooked but still tender, about 10 to 15 minutes.

To serve, slice squid into bite-sized pieces and toss with cilantro leaves.
Serves 10 as a side dish.

asian accents

curried flavors

This home is a perfect example of Occident meets Orient. The occupants of the house returned to live in Asia for the second time and knew exactly what to bring with them. In fact, the table from the restaurant where the husband proposed has followed them everywhere, and has a place of prominence in their foyer. It is no surprise therefore that anniversaries are a cause for celebration in this home. Special occasions such as birthdays and anniversaries are a great excuse to host a intimate dinner with those special people in your life.

The celebrations begin at the bar overlooking the enclosed courtyard. Get the evening off to a tasty start with pappadums and raita. A celebration means fun and to put people in the right mood, the dining table has been set with special sparkle and decorated with silver table accessories and silver placemats. Antique Cambodian and Thai silver boxes are filled with pink roses, and silver beads and ribbons are wrapped around napkins. Don't be afraid to be creative, this table is a festive cornucopia of styles and colors. Cross cultural boundaries with your decor: Here we've mixed Cambodian and Thai silver boxes with modern frosted glass plates. Metallic pens, which are readily available from stationary stores, have been used to decorate the name cards. The custom-made "lazy suzan" has been decorated with tulips and roses. Just before guests arrive, fragrant rose petals are scattered on the table like confetti. A round table makes conversation easy and you don't have to worry about whom you seat at the head. The lights have been dimmed and two Lozal dolls, handmade by Tibetan monks, observe the festivities. A lavish Indian meal awaits the guests.

ethnic chic

cajun to asian

left *The large hand-painted screen adds a striking bolt of color to the room and breaks up the large space, creating an intimate corner for conversation.*

below right *A mass of dried willow branches fans out from the tall woven basket used as a vase; the sharp twisted forms contrast with the smooth simple shapes of the bowls displayed on top of the wooden cabinet.*

The rich, sumptuous colors and textures of Africa and the Orient come together in a celebration of styles in this exotically furnished home.

Deep earth tones and ocher yellows weave their way through the batiks of Indonesia and dance across the primitive paintings that decorate the walls. Handcarved furnishings made from rare wood sit like sculptures amid the flickering light of the candles. Freshly cut giant heliconia and ginger, exotic tropical flowers brought in from nearby Malaysia, scent the warm night air and add a touch of mystery to the evening's atmosphere.

Natural materials have been used to furnish and decorate this room; the dining table centerpiece of yellow orchids seems to sprout naturally from a sculpted iron boat, setting the scene for a casual but chic dinner with friends.

left *Each place setting is highlighted with flowers in tiny vases that have been individually wrapped in batik. Asia has a wide variety of beautiful hand-made fabrics which can be incorporated into your decorating schemes.*

below *The rather severe and formal beauty of the teak and cane settee from East Java is softened with the addition of warm and comfortable cushions. Marinated olives and slices of daikon combine for simple but flavorsome hors d'oeuvres.*

Drawing on the exotic yet urbane appeal of the interior, a chic sit-down dinner has been created that starts in Asia, goes to New Orleans, and then back to Asia for a refreshing dessert. Light hors d'oeuvres of marinated olives and Japanese daikon slices are served with drinks before dinner, the marinated olives can be bought from your local deli. A spicy gumbo for the main course adds a Cajun touch and is hearty enough to require only rice with it. A luscious lychee mousse completes the meal.

cajun shrimp gumbo

ingredients

3 tablespoons olive oil
2 medium-sized onions, peeled and diced
2 cloves garlic, peeled and chopped finely
1 red bell pepper, peeled, seeds and membranes removed
1 (8-ounce) can peeled tomatoes
2 pounds shrimp, shells, tails and heads removed
4 cups okra, trimmed and chopped
$^1/_2$ teaspoon cayenne or to taste
1 teaspoon dried oregano
$^1/_2$ cup white wine
1 cup chicken stock
Salt and freshly ground black pepper

In a large skillet, heat the olive oil and cook onions and garlic over high heat until onions are wilted, about 3 minutes. Take care not to burn the garlic.

Add the bell peppers, tomatoes, shrimp, okra, cayenne, and oregano and cook for about 3 minutes, stirring frequently. Gently rub the oregano between your palms to release the flavor before adding it.

Add white wine and continue to stir, scraping the bottom of pan. Cook for about 3 minutes. Add chicken stock, reduce heat to a simmer and cover. Simmer for 5 minutes. Salt and pepper to taste. Serve with onion rice.
Serves 6.

presentation: *To serve, place a mound of rice in the center of the plate and spoon the gumbo around it.*

onion rice

ingredients

4 tablespoons olive oil
2 medium onions, diced
3 cups rice
6 cups water
Worcestershire sauce, to taste
Salt

Heat a saucepan and add the oil. Add the onions and cook until lightly browned. Add the rice and stir, coating it with the oil. Add water, the Worcestershire sauce, and salt to taste. Reduce heat to a simmer, cover and cook until the rice is cooked and the water absorbed.
Serves 6.

preparation: *To dice onions, peel and cut the onion in half lengthwise. Trim the top end of the onion but keep the root end intact, it will help to hold the onion together. Place one half of the onion down on the cutting board and make a series of horizontal cuts, parallel to the cutting board, from the top to almost the root end but do not cut through the root. Then make a series of vertical slices, again taking care not to cut the root. Hold the onion firmly and cut crosswise into dice. Discard the root end that is left.*

Cajun Shrimp Gumbo.

lychee mousse with sweet raspberry sauce

ingredients
3 tablespoons water
4 teaspoons plain gelatin powder
2 cups lychee purée (see below)
1¹/4 cups heavy cream or whipping cream

lychee purée
3 cups fresh or canned lychees
2–3 tablespoons confectioners' sugar,
more or less to taste

sweet raspberry sauce
3 cups fresh or frozen raspberries
2–3 tablespoons sugar, or more to taste
Juice of ¹/2 lemon
Makes about ¹/2 cup sauce

Place water in saucepan and sprinkle in gelatin. Gently heat water and stir until gelatin has dissolved. Don't let the water boil. Remove from heat and let cool to lukewarm. Stir in lychee purée and let stand until mixture begins to thicken, about 20 minutes.

Whip cream with an electric mixer until medium peaks form. Stir 2 tablespoons of whipped cream into lychee purée, then fold in remaining whipped cream. Fill molds with mousse and gently tap the bottom against table top to eliminate air bubbles. Chill for at least 4 hours before unmolding.

For lychee purée: If using fresh lychees, peel and cut flesh away from pit. Purée in blender, adding powdered sugar to taste. For canned lychees, drain, omit sugar and blend.

For the sauce: Combine all ingredients in a saucepan and bring to a boil. Reduce heat and simmer until thickened, about 10 minutes. Remove from heat and push sauce through a fine sieve with a spatula to remove seeds. Let cool and transfer to squeeze bottle.

Makes about 3¹/2 cups of mousse or 8 individual (3 fluid-ounce) molds.

presentation: *To serve, unmold mousse onto plate and squeeze raspberry sauce circles around mousse.*

a moonlit courtyard

twilight supper

left *Welcome your guests by hanging Chinese lanterns from the trees outside your house. Or place candles in mini terra-cotta cups to lead the way to the party (see page 124).*

Twilight is the perfect time to unwind with family and friends. When the heat of the day begins to wane and the first stars quietly emerge to decorate the evening sky, it's time to host an outdoor party and experience the end of the day and the beginning of night.

No longer is the barbecue an occasion where badly cooked food, hard seats and insect bites are an accepted part of the evening's offerings. When entertaining moved outdoors, the purveyors of lifestyle goods followed, and now functional and stylish outdoor furniture, cooking equipment and crockery are all readily available in an infinite variety of forms. So, you can now hold your alfresco events, whether they be casual or sophisticated, without sacrificing comfort or style. Dress up your surroundings with rustic curios or statues, and bring the comfort of your living room to your outdoor furniture with bright, tropical print cushions. Remember though, when you are entertaining outdoors, your garden should be the star attraction, not the furniture. Let the scents, colors, and patterns of nature enhance your outdoor entertaining area. Perfume the evening air with the scents of jasmine, frangipani or lilies potted in attractive terra-cotta pots. You can also use these to fill dull corners or to supplement your garden if it is not looking its best.

As night falls, you will need to light your party. Line your patio edges with rows of candles and let their flickering light perform shadow dances on the nearby walls. The magical quality of candlelight adds a touch of festivity to any occasion. The colorful translucent fish lanterns (featured on the following pages) are often carried by children during the Chinese August Moon festival. Placed in the center of a glass table and lit by candles, this school of lantern fish makes a whimsical and charming centerpiece.

Keep the menu simple but interesting. The days of sawdust sausages and limp coleslaw are fortunately behind us; today's outdoor cook presents food that is clean but flavorsome. A crispy salad with something marinated and grilled is ideal. You don't want to be rushing in and out of the house to check on what's cooking indoors. Summer fruits, abundant in flavor and variety, are a cool and easy way to finish the meal.

left *Translucent fish lanterns, often carried by children during the Chinese "Moon" festival in August. Use festive seasonal ornaments such as banners, candles or lanterns from different cultures to bring a fiesta feel to your entertaining.*

above *A Chinese lantern brings a glow to this corner of the court-yard. Look for these bright paper lanterns at stores in your local Chinatown.*

Transform your home into a chic and sultry cocktail lounge. For a wonderfully grown-up party, blend the sophistication of a Manhattan cocktail lounge with the decadence of a scene from the Arabian Nights.

To create the mood, rivers of sheer, colored fabric were hung from the ceiling, the soft cascades of indigo, turquoise and pale green adding an air of fantasy to the occasion. Opulent jewel-toned cushions are scattered invitingly on the sofa for those who prefer quite and intimate conversation to the cocktail party chatter. The Arabian Nights ambience is conjured with colored-glass serving dishes and silver trays set on honeycombed wooden tabletops. Quintessential cocktail party elements were added to finish the lounge look: the martini glass, its cool, elegant shape an icon of 1950s chic (think Cary Grant); bar accessories such as cocktail shakers, swizzle sticks and olives; and cocktail napkins which are the perfect size for those irresistible mouthfuls of fabulous finger food.

This sophisticated look is not difficult to achieve but it does require a little preparation. The Arabian Nights mood was created by hanging layers of sheer fabric around the room curtain-style (see page 125). Once you've gathered your choice of fabric, the rest is easy and well worthwhile doing; the right decor can really make your party one to remember. Most of the finger foods served can be prepared well in advance and are a delicious mix of hot and spicy, and cool and refreshing flavors. Since we are going all out, hire a bartender to mix the drinks and help pass the hors d'oeuvres. This keeps the fun flowing and leaves you free to catch up with your friends; after all, the party is for you too.

For a cocktail party, finger-food size hors d'oeuvres are a must so that your guests have one hand free to hold their drinks. The tangy shrimp dish below is the exception to this rule but it is so good we had to include it anyway. Most of the hors d'oeuvres presented here can be made at least partly in advance, which allows you to spend the maximum time with your guests and have as much fun as everyone else. The flavors here are truly international, from the ginger, cilantro and lime juice redolent of Asia to the sophisticated flavors of Europe.

dill & ginger shrimp starter

ingredients

1 pound shrimp, peeled and deveined
3 slices lemon

marinade

1/2 cup olive oil
2 tablespoons white wine vinegar
3 tablespoons Dijon mustard
1 clove garlic, minced
1 teaspoon or more grated fresh ginger
2 tablespoons chopped fresh dill
Cracked pepper
1/2 teaspoon sugar

Add shrimp and lemon to a pot of boiling water and boil for about 3 minutes or until shrimp is cooked. Take care not to overcook the shrimp or it will become tough. Drain shrimp thoroughly and let cool.

For the marinade:
Whisk together marinade ingredients. Add shrimp to marinade and mix together until shrimp is coated. Refrigerate until ready to serve.
Serves 8–10 as hors d'oeuvre-sized servings.

note: *This dish can be made one day ahead and also makes a wonderful starter. Simply place some marinated shrimp over mixed greens and serve as a salad course.*

parmesan stars

ingredients

1 1/2 cups Parmigiano-Reggiano cheese, finely grated
1 cup ricotta cheese
1 cup finely diced onion (slightly less than 1 large onion)
2 tablespoons cream
12 slices white bread, crusts removed

Preheat oven to 425 ° F.

Mix cheeses, onion and cream together. Spread 1 heaped tablespoon of the cheese mixture onto each slice of bread until the surface is evenly covered. Cut each slice into 4 triangular pieces and place on a baking sheet. Bake for 10–15 minutes or until golden brown and serve.
Makes about 48 mini toasts.

presentation: *For the festive presentation shown here, use a star-shaped cutter to cut out toasts. Spread cheese mixture onto bread, carefully cut out shapes with cutter and bake.*

preparation: *The cheese mixture can be made a day in advance and refrigerated.*

Fabulous Finger Food.

spiced nuts

ingredients

3/4 teaspoon cayenne
1/2 teaspoon curry powder
1/2 teaspoon salt
1/4 teaspoon ground coriander
1/4 teaspoon ground cinnamon
1/4 teaspoon ground ginger
2 tablespoons vegetable oil
2 cups shelled whole almonds or cashews

Preheat oven to 325 ° F.

Mix together all the dry ingredients except the nuts in a small bowl and set aside. Heat the oil in a skillet, preferably a nonstick one. Add the spice mixture and stir well. Cook until fragrant, about 1 minute. Place the nuts in a bowl, add the spice mixture, and toss well. Spread the nuts in a single layer on a baking sheet. Bake until fragrant, about 15 minutes. Remove the baking sheet from the oven and toss nuts with any spices and oil that have accumulated on the pan. Sprinkle with more salt if desired. Let nuts cool to room temperature.

Makes 2 cups.

note: *Nuts can be stored in an airtight container for up to a week.*

cheesy mushroom treats

ingredients

30 button mushrooms, stems removed
4 ounces brie cheese
1 small jar of sundried tomatoes packed in olive oil

Preheat oven to 425 ° F.

Cut brie into 30 pieces. Drain the sundried tomatoes and cut into 30 pieces.

Place mushroom caps upside down on a baking sheet. Stuff hollow part of the caps with brie and then sundried tomatoes. Place in the oven and bake until the cheese has melted, about 7 minutes As you transfer mushroom caps to the serving tray, gently blot the bottom on a paper towel to remove the liquid which has accumulated during baking. *Makes 30.*

note: *The mushroom caps can be stuffed, covered and refrigerated the night before. Just pop in hot oven to bake before serving.*

persian rolls

ingredients

3 (10 x 10-inch) frozen puff pastry sheets
9 gherkins
36 thin slices of sopressa salami, or any other salami of your choice

Preheat oven to 425 ° F.

Cut the pastry sheets in half. Cut each half into 3 even pieces lengthwise, resulting in 18 rectangles. Then make a diagonal cut across each rectangle. You should end up with 36 triangles.

Quarter gherkins lengthwise until you have about 36 quarters.

Place a triangle of puff pastry on your work surface with the wide end toward you. Place a slice of salami at the base end and top with a gherkin slice. Roll the wide end of the pastry around the salami and gherkin and continue rolling toward the point end. Place on a baking sheet with point-side down.

Bake until pastry is golden and puffed, 10 to 15 minutes.
Serves 6.

note: *The rolls can be made the day before and refrigerated. Bake before serving.*

Cheesy Mushroom Treats.

beef salad on cucumber slices

ingredients

dressing

2 tablespoons lime juice

1 tablespoon rice vinegar

1 tablespoon fish sauce (nam pla)

1 tablespoon sugar

2 bird's eye chilies, or more to taste, chopped

1/4 cup chopped mint leaves

1/4 cup chopped cilantro leaves

8 ounces very thinly sliced roast beef from the deli counter, torn into bite-size pieces

3 to 4 large cucumbers, peeled

For the dressing: whisk together lime juice, vinegar, fish sauce, sugar, and chilies in a bowl, until the sugar is dissolved. Toss beef with lime dressing and let stand for at least 15 minutes, or cover and refrigerate overnight. Just before serving, toss mint and cilantro with beef mixture.

Cut cucumbers crosswise into $1/2$-inch-thick slices. Using a melon baller, scoop out a pocket from the center of each cucumber slice. Top each cucumber slice with a teaspoon of the beef mixture.

Makes about 30 slices.

presentation: *For a different presentation, use a cookie cutter to cut shapes from cucumber slices while discarding the peel at the same time. Choose a cutter which is just slightly smaller than the circumference of the cucumber slice. Cut cucumber into slices, then use cutter to cut shapes out of each slice.*

measurement *and* conversion tables

Measurements in this book are given in volume as far as possible. Teaspoon, tablespoon and cup measurements should be level, not heaped, unless otherwise indicated. Australian readers please note that the standard Australian measuring spoon is larger than the UK or American spoon by 5 ml, so use only $^3/4$ tablespoon when following the recipes.

liquid conversions

Imperial	Metric	US cups
$^1/2$ fl oz	15 ml	1 tablespoon
1 fl oz	30 ml	$^1/8$ cup
2 fl oz	60 ml	$^1/4$ cup
4 fl oz	125 ml	$^1/2$ cup
5 fl oz ($^1/4$ pint)	150 ml	$^2/3$ cup
6 fl oz	175 ml	$^3/4$ cup
8 fl oz	250 ml	1 cup
12 fl oz	375 ml	1$^1/2$ cups
16 fl oz	500 ml	2 cups

Note:
    1 UK pint = 20 fl oz
    1 US pint = 16 fl oz

solid weight conversions

Imperial	Metric
$^1/2$ oz	15 g
1 oz	30g
1$^1/2$ oz	50 g
2 oz	60 g
3 oz	90 g
3$^1/2$ oz	100 g
4 oz ($^1/4$ lb)	125 g
5 oz	150 g
6 oz	185 g
7 oz	200 g
8 oz ($^1/2$ lb)	250 g
9 oz	280 g
10 oz	300 g
16 oz (1 lb)	500 g (0.5 kg)
32 oz (2 lb)	1 kg

oven temperatures

Heat	Fahrenheit	Centigrade/Celsius	British Gas Mark
Very cool	225	110	1/4
Cool or slow	275–300	135–150	1–2
Moderate	350	175	4
Hot	425	220	7
Very hot	450	230	8

Index of recipes

appetizers
-Beef Salad on Cucumber Slices   121
-Cheesy Mushroom Treats   120
-Cherry Tomatoes Stuffed with Crabmeat   72
-Cilantro Crab Cakes   80
-Daikon Maki   70
-Dill and Ginger Shrimp Starter   118
-Easy Popiah   32
-Marinated Olives   98
-Mushroom Satay   82
-Parmesan Stars   118
-Persian Rolls   120
-Puff Pastry Canapés   53
-Roasted Squid   83
-Sesame Style Salmon Tartare   72
-Shrimp Noodle Rolls   108
-Smoked Salmon Ribbons   51
-Spicy Madeira Beef Puffs   52
-Spicy Pork Bundles   108
-Spring Rolls   62
-Vegetable Curry Puffs   50

beef
-Beef Salad on Cucumber Slices   121
-Beef Tenderloin   22
-Spicy Madeira Beef Puffs   52
bell peppers
-Cajun Shrimp Gumbo   98
-Caponata   22
bread
-Colonial Tuna Sandwiches   50
-Parmesan Stars   118

Cajun Shrimp Gumbo   98
Caponata   22
cheese
-Caper-Cream Cheese Spread   51
-Cheesy Mushroom Treats   120
-Cherry Tomatoes Stuffed with Crabmeat   72
-Ginger and Orange Cream   23
-Parmesan Stars   118
Cherry Tomatoes Stuffed with Crabmeat   72
chicken
- Chicken Rice   34
-Chicken Satay   80
-Creamy Cardamom Chicken   90
Chili Sauce   33
Chocolate Dipped Fruit   35
cilantro
-Cilantro Crab Cakes   80
Colonial Tuna Sandwiches   50
cream
-Green Tea Ice Cream   45

-Lychee Mousse with Sweet Raspberry Sauce   99
-Parmesan Stars   118
-Pumpkin Soup   42
Creamy Cardamom Chicken   90
cucumber
-Beef Salad on Cucumber Slices   121
-Pineapple and Cucumber Salsa   82
-Raita   90
-Smoked Salmon Ribbons   51

Daikon Maki   70
Daikon Slices   98
desserts
-Chocolate Dipped Fruit   35
-Fruit Salad with a Ginger and Orange Cream   23
-Green Tea Ice Cream   45
-Indian Ice Cream   91
-Lychee Mousse with Sweet Raspberry Sauce   99
-Mangosteen Sorbet   110
Dill and Ginger Shrimp Starter   118

Easy Popiah   32
eggplant
-Caponata   22

fish
-Grilled Balsamic and Soy Salmon   110
-Sesame Style Salmon Tartare   72
-Smoked Salmon Ribbons   51
fruit
-Chocolate Dipped Fruit   35
-Fruit Salad with Ginger and Orange Cream   23
-Lychee Mousse with Sweet Raspberry Sauce   99
-Mangosteen Sorbet   110
-Pineapple and Cucumber Salsa   82
-Pork Loin with Mango Salsa and Raspberry Sauce   44
-Soursop Daiquiries   63
Fruit Salad with a Ginger and Orange Cream   23

ginger
-Dill and Ginger Shrimp Starter   118
-Ginger and Orange Cream   23
- Pickled Ginger   73
Green Tea Ice Cream   45
Grilled Balsamic and Soy Salmon   110

Indian Ice Cream   91

Lychee Mousse with Sweet Raspberry Sauce   99

mango
-Pork Loin with Mango Salsa and Raspberry Sauce   44
-Soursop Daiquiries   63
Mangosteen Sorbet   110
Marinated Olives   98

mayonnaise
-Colonial Tuna Sandwiches   50
mushrooms
-Cheesy Mushroom Treats   120
-Mushroom Satay   82
-Sautéed Shiitake Mushrooms   44
-Spicy Madeira Beef Puffs   52
Mushroom Satay   82

noodles
-Shrimp Noodle Rolls   108

okra
-Cajun Shrimp Gumbo   98
-Okra with Mustard Seeds   90
olives
-Caponata   22
-Marinated Olives   98
Onion Rice   98

Pappadums   90
Parmesan Stars   118
pastry
-Persian Rolls   120
-Puff Pastry Canapés   53
-Spicy Madeira Beef Puffs   52
-Vegetable Curry Puffs   50
Pickled Ginger   73
Pineapple and Cucumber Salsa   82
pork
-Easy Popiah   32
-Pork Loin with Mango Salsa and Raspberry Sauce   44
-Spicy Pork Bundles   108
-Spring Rolls   62
Puff Pastry Canapés   53
Pumpkin Soup   42

Raita   90
rice
-Chicken Rice   34
-Daikon Maki   70
-Onion Rice   98
-Sushi Rice   71
-Wild Rice   111
Roasted Squid   83

salads   see vegetables
Salad with Lime Dressing   109
Satay Sauce   81
sauces, salsas, spreads, condiments and dressings
-Caper-Cream Cheese Spread   51
-Chili Sauce   33
-Ginger and Orange Cream   23
-Calamansi Lime Dressing   109
-Mango Salsa   44

-Pineapple and Cucumber Salsa   82
-Raita   90
-Raspberry Sauce   44
-Satay Sauce   81
-Sesame Dressing   72
-Soy Balsamic Sauce   110
-Sweet Raspberry Sauce   99
Sautéed Shiitake Mushrooms   44
seafood   see also fish
-Cajun Shrimp Gumbo   98
-Cherry Tomatoes Stuffed with Crabmeat   72
-Cilantro Crab Cakes   80
-Dill and Ginger Shrimp Starter   118
-Roasted Squid   83
-Shrimp Noodle Rolls   108
Sesame Style Salmon Tartare   72
shrimp
-Cajun Shrimp Gumbo   98
-Dill and Ginger Shrimp Starter   118
-Shrimp Noodle Rolls   108
Smoked Salmon Ribbons   51
soup
-Pumpkin Soup   42
Soursop Daiquiries   63
Spiced Nuts   119
Spicy Madeira Beef Puffs   52
Spring Rolls   62
Steamed Baby Kai-lan   43
Sushi Rice   71

tomatoes
-Cajun Shrimp Gumbo   98
-Caponata   22
-Cherry Tomatoes Stuffed with Crabmeat   72

vegetables, salads   see also individual vegetables
-Caponata   22
-Cheesy Mushroom Treats   120
-Mushroom Satay   82
-Okra with Mustard Seeds   90
-Pickled Ginger   73
-Pineapple and Cucumber Salsa   82
-Pumpkin Soup   42
-Salad with Lime Dressing   109
-Sautéed Shiitake Mushrooms   44
-Steamed Baby Kai-lan   43
-Vegetable Curry Puffs   50

Wild Rice   111
wine
-Cajun Shrimp Gumbo   98

yogurt
-Creamy Cardamom Chicken   90
-Raita   90